Barry Fantoni

Who is he?
Writer, cartoonist, actor, poet,
playwright, painter, etcher, chef,
gourmet, vegetarian, satirist,
wit, Jew, gigolo, compere, musician,
Christian, philosopher, orator,
journalist, philanthropist,
traveller, dandy? All of these, and
yet none of them.
How does one sum up a star?
How do we explain the scent of
summer roses?
Perhaps it is best left to history
to pay its own, unimpeachable
tribute to the man we call
Bargy Fontapi.

D1343716

"But it's a milestone in the history of British Art, man."

PRIVATE EYE

Cartoon Library 5

100 best jokes of

Barry
Fantoni

A Private Eye Book with
André Deutsch, London.
Also published in this series:
Michael Heath, Hector Breeze, Larry,
and Martin Honeysett.

A Private Eye Book with Andre Deutsch London.
Also published in this series:
Michael Heath, Hector Breeze, Larry and Martin Honeysett.

Published in Great Britain 1975 by
Private Eye Productions Limited,
34 Greek Street, London W1.
In association with Andre Deutsch Limited,
105 Great Russell Street, London WC1.

©Pressdram Limited and The Listener.
SBN 233 966803
Some of the following cartoons were drawn specially for
this book, most were first seen in Private Eye and The Listener.

Designed by Peter Windett.
Printed in Great Britain by Leo Thorpe Limited.

"Christ man, I give enough for it already!"

"Pru, what a scorcher!"

"I'm setting my nervous breakdown to music".

"I know, let's play Policeman's Knock!"

'SMOKE?'

".....and a little man from the village delivers our vegetables."

"I loved your single, man"

"Kevin's just killed his first policeman"

'So Mad Dick, Crazy Chris, and Nasty Ned
gang-banged Dirty Doreen, and they all lived happily ever after'

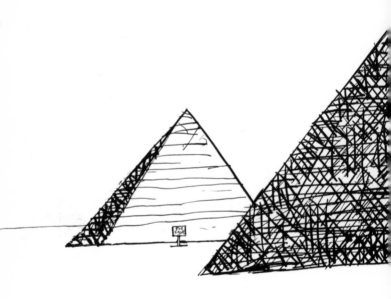

"This pyramid selling has got out of hand"

"Are you gone here often?"

"The country's going to the pigs!"

'Have you got something for a long-haired git?'

'Er, what do you mean "Easter", man?'

1.

'Just a bit over, madam?'

"Slimline tonic!"

'GRATE!'

There's something interesting in tomorrow's

TIMES

"Damn it, and I went and bought today's".

'Is this a Degas I see before me?'

"It's his old steam radio."

'I've sat around on floors all night more times than you've had hot dinners'

"GOT ANY WEEDS, MAN ?"

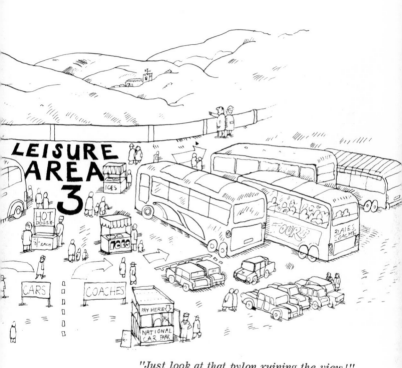

"Just look at that pylon ruining the view!"

'Hello, it's the collective unconscious!'

"I'd love to make it with you Brenda, but
I don't think it would be worth all the
bother."

"60 - 70 - 80 - Phew, what a scorcher!"

"I've got this fantastic idea for an idea, man

"Hello, man."

'England Expects That Every Man Will Do His Thing!'

"Kindly leave the sage."

"Haven't you got anything dangerous ?"

'In those days I could only afford one square meal a day'

'I'm not boring you am I?'

"I've just sprinkled my flowers man,
and I can't do a thing with them".

" Great, man."

"There's not much on the television tonight."

"I hope you are not going to engage me in conversation."

"Sorry man, I'm not here."

'Frankly, Roy, I think they're taking this Forties thing a bit too far'

"I see Nancy Mitford has passed over "

'Can you move the sight screens?'

'Help you carry it for a few bob, guv?'

'*Dear Diary, FRI: Punch up with fuzz at pop festival*
SAT: Punch up with fuzz at football match
SUN: Punch up with fuzz at National Front demo'

" I'm a Gas Man!"

"Violence, lovely violence!"

'Hello! That pub's new'

*'I'm campaigning for Greater Personal Privacy.
I wonder if I could come in a minute'*

"I'm sorry, he's busy clearing his desk"

"You weigh twelve stone and thirteen ounces."

'Where there's Munch there's Monet'

THIS FRIEND OF
MINE GAVE UP
CARBOHYDRATES
AND HER
BRAIN
BECAME
COMPLETELY
MENTALLY
AFFECTED.

"A guinea for your thoughts, man".

"How do you know I've got a broken leg when you can't even speak English ?"

"You ought to have this one recycled, Squire"

"This could be the start of something small"

B. DEMPSTER
CERTIFIED
ACCOUNTANT

1.

'Excuse me, do you know anywhere we can get a Spanish meal?'

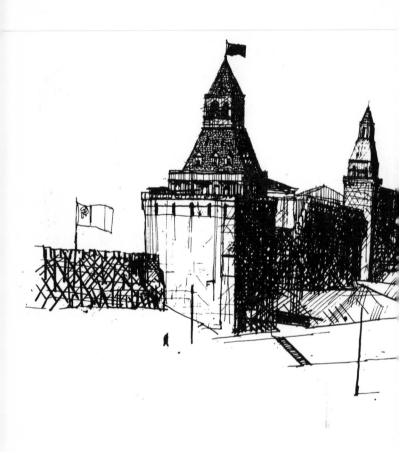

HOT
RUNNING
DOGS

"You're fired!"

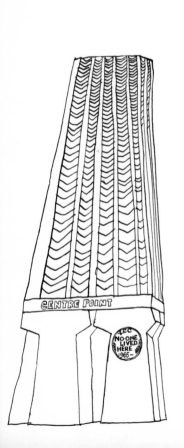

CENTRE POINT

LCC
NO-ONE
LIVED
HERE
1965–

KEEP OFF
THE GRASS

'It's all over bar the shooting'

"OK, keep your vest on!"

"I see the bottom's dropped out of Renoir."

'Have you got something for the man who's living with my mother?'